Millicent the Magnificent

Written and photographed by:

Diane Baxter Trapeni

ISBN: 9798635993835

Keep an eye out for these other exciting titles:

Nellie the Nibbler

Alice the Guinea Pig

Penny the Python

Jeremiah, a Song Bird

Vincent

Hubert

Phil Harmonic

Jeff Sticks up for his Buddies

Cord, Glue and 8 Screws

A Three Piggie Circus

DEDICATION

To my beautiful niece, Emerald, who makes my heart soar to heights I never knew existed! I love you!

DMBT

"I believe in you!" Millicent used to say

to the children in her art classes.

"You can, if you think you can!"

she'd sing to the little ones.

"You are WONDERFUL!" she'd gush enthusiastically...and because she believed, they began to see it, too. Millicent was not only a teacher, but a coach, a cheerleader and above all, a true friend.

Mylinda, the giraffe, always said so.
Marge, the hippo, agreed and Simon, the skunk, seconded it! These buddies all grew up together, you see.

Life wasn't always easy but it wasn't hard either because they had each other to rely on. Whenever any one of them felt down, being together lifted them up and in the process, new art work was born!

Sure, they all had their own lives and other friends but what they all had in common was a love for Millicent.

Millicent was an art therapist.
Art was the way she connected with others.
When her clients delved into their art, their stresses melted away.
Smiles came back and friendship bonds were formed.

Clients would come to her for comfort. They would draw and paint whatever came to them and then they would leave happier, calmer and richer.

Lots of her clients became artists, too.
They went from homeless, hopeless and penniless to hopeful, happy and sometimes rich and famous!
YES, ALWAYS RICHER!

Millicent was not your usual art therapist. Oh No!
She's not what you'd expect.

She teaches from a tank...
an aquarium, really...
One as large as a room...
a room-sized aquarium in a
museum to be exact.
Millicent is an octopus!

Lots of arms…

Lots of hugs…

Lots of love to give…and BIG smiles!

She's always in motion it seems.

(It's probably the water moving…Do you feel woozy?)

Her best buddies call her, "Millicent the Magnificent!" "Simon," said Marge. "Remember the first day we all met Millie?" "Yeah, we were on a school field trip and Millie was the main attraction!" Simon reminisced.

Marge snickered. "Yeah, she was just beginning her art thing then.

"Now look at her!"
"Millicent is World renowned!"

"She's a famous author of art books!"

She'll probably win the Nobel
Peace Prize some day!"
added Mylinda.

Yes, Millicent was the catalyst.

She brought people together to do things they

NEVER knew were possible.

Over her tank were the words,

"You can, if you think you can!"

And they did.

The End

(of wondering and the beginning of making

your dreams a reality!)

Keep an eye out for these other exciting Children's Books:

Penny the Enormous Python

Floyd the Colorful Chameleon

Francesca the Tropical Red-eyed Green Frog

Joe's Got Spots

Merrill the Squirrel and Jen the Hen:

Part 6 Brittany's Back!!!

Sydney (Cat)

Alice the Guinea Pig

Frances, a Gifted Frog for Sure!

Saffire. (Butterfly)

Serendipity. (Fish)

Jeremiah, the Song Bird

Christmas at the Castle

We are proud to introduce:

Jules' Sleep Over

Jules loves his cousin Simon but…

Jules will not break the rules for anyone…

not even his best friend and cousin, Simon.

Would you?

Also, introducing, Kathleen Fox, the magnificent artist!

Kathleen made Jules and Simon come alive!

About the TrapStone LLC: Owner and Author…

My name is Miss Diane. I taught for 42

years and have read thousands of books

aloud to children.

I enjoyed that so much, I decided to write

and illustrate books for you myself.

Enjoy!!!

About the TrapStone LLC: Manager…

Ken Stone Sr. is a computer programmer and a business partner extraordinaire. He put my words, pictures and computer magic together so you could meet, Millicent the Magnificent.